There's a poet behind you...

Edited by Morag Styles and Helen Cook
Illustrated by Caroline Holden

A & C Black · London

© 1988 A&C Black (Publishers) Limited

Published by A&C Black (Publishers) Ltd
35 Bedford Row, London WC1R 4JH

British Library Cataloguing in Publication Data

There's a poet behind you.
1. Poetry
I. Styles, Morag II. Cook, Helen
808.1

ISBN 0-7136-3056-6

Filmset by August Filmsetting, Haydock, St Helens
Printed in Great Britain at The Bath Press

Contents

About this Book
Morag Styles and Helen Cook   4

Journey to a Poem
Grace Nichols   6

Dogs, Banana Milkshakes
and other Secrets of Poetry
Adrian Mitchell   24

Taking a Word for a Walk
Gillian Clarke   54

While Greasy Joan
Doth Keel the Pot
Michael Rosen   80

The Poem Business
John Agard   106

The Poets and their Books   120

About this Book

Would you like to know some of the secrets of poetry?

In this book five poets share some of their secrets with you. They tell you why they write and how they write. They give you a taste of their poetry and tell you a bit about themselves. You may get ideas for writing or just enjoy reading what they have to say.

You might have been told that poetry is good for you, but as **Michael Rosen** explains later, 'We're not interested in prisons where children are forced to listen to poems'. Poetry is about discovery, it's about making words valuable, sorting things out, sharing ideas and it's also for enjoyment, making people laugh and having fun.

But it isn't always easy – 'I've written some stinkers' says **Adrian Mitchell**. And, you must write about things you care about. He puts it like this:

> Don't write about Autumn
> 'Cos that's the season
> Write your poems
> For a real reason

We invited these poets to write for you because they show the different things poetry can do. **John Agard** describes how an idea for a poem is like an electric switch. You fit together feelings, pictures, dreams, happenings with words instead of wires to make the electricity, but it's the idea which switches on the poem.

Grace Nichols tells you that she was 'awakened by tropical things' and that a poem has a living spirit of its own.

Gillian Clarke shows you how to take a word for a walk – words with music in them like 'pandemonium' or 'Diego Maradonna'.

Each poet has a different way of getting to a poem, but they all need to write about the things which matter to them: funny things; times when they're scared or worried or just plain happy; moments when they feel really strongly; times when they're confused and writing a poem helps to make sense of the muddle.

This is a book to carry round in your bag, take to school, read lying on your bed or on the bus. You might lend it to your parents, your sisters and brothers, your friends or your teacher; but don't lose it, it will help you find your way on the journey to a poem.

Helen Cook
Morag Styles

Grace Nichols

'My own imagination is stirred
by my childhood. I was
awakened by tropical things.'

Grace Nichols

Journey to a Poem

Whenever I remember the country village along the Guyana coast, where I spent my small-girl days, I can't help seeing water water everywhere. Brown silky water when it rained heavily. Fish swimming into people's yards and children catching them in old baskets. One of the best memories I have of myself is standing up to my calves in the sunlit water, watching the shapes of fish go by and every now and then cupping my own hands underneath and feeling the slippery fish slip through my fingers. My favourite fish was the sunfish. It was a little longer than some of the other fishes, with a fine grey scale on top and a reddish orange glow of a belly below.

But the nice thing about Highdam, that was the name of the village, was that the water in the yards and pastures never stayed on the land for too long because there were these two kokers with big wheels on either side of the village bridge. Workmen would go and turn the wheels, which always made me think of windmills, until bit by bit the water drained away into a canal at the back of the village. Then the hot sun would soon make everything dry and children could run around again playing their cricket and rounders and hopscotch.

Another Highdam thing I remember is sneaking down to the seashore with my sisters and brother to catch crab in the early mornings, just before the last bit of darkness disappeared from the skies.

But you must be wondering what all this has to do with poetry.

Well, my childhood life in that country village plays a big part in my poetry because a lot of my poems are about creatures and back-home happenings. Just as how your own imagination might be stirred by thoughts of winter for example – of crunching through thick powdery snow, tobogganning, making a snow man, maybe curling up in front of fires with a hot drink – so my own imagination is stirred by my childhood. I was awakened by tropical things:

I am a Parrot

I'm a parrot
I live in a cage
I'm nearly always
in a vex-up rage

I used to fly
all light and free
in the luscious
green forest canopy

I'm a parrot
I live in a cage
I'm nearly always
in a vex-up rage

I miss the wind
against my wing
I miss the nut
and the fruit picking

I'm a parrot
I live in a cage
I'm nearly always
in a vex-up rage

I squawk I talk
I curse I swear
I repeat the things
I shouldn't hear

So don't come near me
or put out your hand
because I'll pick you
if I can

    pickyou
    pickyou
    if I can
I want to be free
CAN'T YOU UNDERSTAND

No television but a lot of friends

When I was a little girl in Guyana we didn't have television (though Guyana has television now), so people had to find their own enjoyment. Our house was always full of friends who would visit us at night, sometimes just to talk stories. I would love being in the midst of everything. When they started to tell jumbie stories (ghost stories) there I'd be sitting, hanging on to every word, feeling the goose pimples on my skin.

I Like to Stay Up

I like to stay up
and listen
when big people talking
jumbie stories

OoooooooooH
I does feel so tingly
and excited
inside me

But when my mother say
'Girl, time for bed'
then is when
I does feel a dread
then is when
I does jump into me bed
then is when I does cover up
from me feet to me head

then is when
I does wish
I didn't listen
to no stupid jumbie story
then is when
I does wish
I did read me book instead

Grandmothers

Grandmothers are grand mothers even if they spoil
us just a little bit by slipping us an extra piece of
homemade fudge when no one is looking. I remember following my Grandma to collect her old age
pension when I was growing up and she would sit
patiently and allow me to brush her soft silvery hair
and put it in all kinds of styles. So it wasn't surprising that I wrote a poem about grandmother and
hair.

Granny Granny Please Comb my Hair

Granny Granny
please comb my hair
you always take your time
you always take such care

You put me to sit on a cushion
between your knees
you rub a little coconut oil
parting gentle as a breeze

Mummy Mummy
she's always in a hurry-hurry rush
she pulls my hair
sometimes she tugs

But Granny
you have all the time in the world
and when you're finished
you always turn my head and say
'Now, who's a nice girl'

Of course a poet doesn't only get ideas for poems from childhood, or is only inspired by that. Ideas from poems come from all about, sometimes when you least expect them to. Like sitting at the laundrette one day, shortly after coming to England, and watching the clothes go around in the tumble drier.

Tumble Drying at the Laundrette

Spin spin spin
tumble tumble tumble
bigs and smalls
shorts and talls
all go round and round

Spin spin spin
tumble tumble tumble
zip-ups and cottons
woollies and buttons
all go round and round

Sometimes you get ideas from what people say. I got an idea for a poem this way. I was having a chat with a friend of mine and she was telling me something about her little nephew called Peter, who she said loved bananas. One day he was sitting at the table when he suddenly banged his spoon and announced, 'I'm a banana man,' because his mother had given him something to eat that he didn't like. That line, 'I'm a banana man' immediately started to jump around in my head. What a lovely line I thought. 'I'm a banana man, I'm a banana man.' Sometimes when you get an idea for a poem in your head, it keeps haunting you. Some ideas are more pushy than others. This idea just kept buzzing around in my head saying please, please write me. I just had to sit down as soon as I got home and write the poem, *I'm a Banana Man* for Peter. As I was writing this poem I was saying it aloud. I think poems, especially poems for children, should not only be read on the page but should be said out aloud too, to hear and taste all the sounds and rhythms in the poem.

I'm a Banana Man

I'm a banana man
I just love shaking
those yellow hands
yes man

Banana in the morning
Banana in the evening
Banana before I go to bed
at night, that's right
that's how much I love
the Banana Bite

I'm a banana man
not a Superman
or a Batman
or a Spiderman
no man

Banana in the morning
Banana in the evening
Banana before I go to bed
at night, that's right
that's how much I love
the Banana Bite

As I said, I wrote the banana poem the very day I
got the idea for it, but some ideas and the poems
that develop from them are more patient and might
sometimes take years before they're written. Take
for example my poem, *For Forest*. I wrote this poem
about a year ago while lying in bed one morning
right here in England. But the roots of this poem
began some twelve years ago in the heart of the
Guyanan forests.

Most Guyanese never see the forests or jungle
because the majority of people live in towns and
villages along the Guyana coast which runs
alongside the Atlantic. I was very lucky to get the
chance to spend some time in the interior of our
ruggedly beautiful country. We travelled by
Landrover, by boat, by helicopter, plane and by
foot. We sailed down dark mysterious rivers,
bathed in creeks, crossed rapids, saw spectacular
waterfalls – some changing colours in the rays of the
sunlight. It was the most exciting journey of my
life.

I will never forget the night we spent at 'Mountain Top' – the name the Amerindian people, the first native people of the Americas, gave to this particularly steep mountain. We could only get to the top of the mountain by helicopter and spent the night sleeping on makeshift little wooden beds under a tent with all the sides open. It was a night of thunder and lightning. As I lay on my bed staring into the darkness of the forest, the crackling purple lightning kept lighting up the huge tree trunks around our tents. I had heard stories of lightning splitting trees and was terrified by the thought that a massive forest tree might fall on our tent. I also kept imagining the eyes of a jaguar staring at me through the darkness. But I survived that night and loved every minute of the rest of my stay.

But why didn't I write a poem for forest right there and then in the forest? Why did the poem suddenly come one morning while lying in bed under my warm quilt, twelve years later. This is one of the mysteries of poetry and of the imagination. As I lay there the whole feel of the forest came back to me for no apparent reason – the density, the aerial roots hanging down, the waterfalls, the mystery of what could be hiding in the thick undergrowth of those trees.

For Forest

Forest could keep secrets
Forest could keep secrets

Forest tune in everyday
To watersound and birdsound
Forest letting her hair down
to the teaming creeping of her forest-ground

but Forest don't broadcast her business
No, Forest cover her business down
from sky and fast-eye sun
and when night come
and darkness wrap her like a gown
Forest is a bad dream woman

Forest dreaming about mountain
and when earth was young
Forest dreaming of the caress of gold
Forest rootsing with mysterious Eldorado

And when howler monkey
wake her up with howl
Forest just stretch and stir
to a new day of sound

but coming back to secrets
Forest could keep secrets
Forest could keep secrets

    And we must keep Forest

Reading back the poem I was surprised at the line, 'And we must keep Forest' because, in a way, it reflects my own concern about the preservation of our forests. But I didn't set out to say this at all in my poem. I wasn't thinking of making people aware of the importance of keeping our forests. It just came out in the poem. This is what makes poetry exciting for me. A poet can discover things in her own poetry. It's like going on an adventure. You don't know quite where the poem will take you because it has a living mind or spirit of its own. So one of the most important things in writing a poem is to tune into the feelings of the poem, to listen to that still small voice in the poem, instead of forcing it to say the things you think you ought to say.

Be true to your imagination

Nobody can make you into a poet but if you love words – if certain words or expressions make you laugh; feel sad; get very excited; leave you in goose pimples or just make you feel plain happy then you have the 'potential' – you have it within you to become a poet, because you're deeply moved by words. But you might be moved just as deeply by music or dancing or painting. So being moved isn't enough. Poets write because they can't stop themselves from writing, even if they wanted to.

If you ever find yourself writing a poem, be true to your imagination. Tune into the poem and write what you really feel and imagine, no matter how ridiculous you think this might sound to someone else. I remember reading a poem one day in which a small boy pointed to a fly, flying around the wall, and told his father, 'little bird'. I was so struck by that because I had never in all my life seen a fly as a 'little bird'. But why not? Both have wings. Both can fly.

Poetry helps us to see the world through new eyes. Seeing the world through the eyes of the boy — instead of just seeing a fly, we too can suddenly see a little bird. We can even see the world through the eyes of a poem itself:

The Dis-satisfied Poem

I'm a dissatisfied poem
    I really am
there's so many things
    I don't understand
like why I'm lying
    on this flat white page
when there's so much to do
    in the world out there
But sometimes when I catch a glimpse
    of the world outside
it makes my blood curl
    it makes me want to stay inside
and hide
    please turn me quick
before I cry
    they would hate it if I wet the pages

Here are some children's poems about the night, which have a similar flavour to Grace Nichols' poem *I Like to Stay Up*.

Darkness In The Night

    A whiskery shadow illuminates
    on a wall   it is a tree
    with its spiky fingers gliding
    silently
    over my bed, boards are creaking
    I think there is a fiery dragon
    Breathing, but it is only my
    Brother turning over a page
    In his book. I look out of my
    window and a thousand
    Eyes are looking at me but it is
    Only the lights of the town.
    This is how I get frightened.   Ben, 8

I am lying in
my bed
I am frightened
There are pictures
on the wall
of tigers and lions
which
are alive
and roaring.
I see shapes and shadows
on the wall
and the
trees tapping the
window
as I lie in my bed
I am frightened.

Elizabeth, 8

My Midnight Garden

TICK, TICK, TICK,
A clock counts away the night hours
I draw my curtains back to reveal
A mysterious black land
The outlines of trees, bushes, shrubs
Standing in the grim shroud of the dark
Corners veiled in the black shadow
    of the kingdom of the dark.

The only thing that is moving
Is the gentle swaying of the trees.
A black outline is caught by
    the shadows of the moon
Which light up a silvery tint
    to the blackness of the night.
Tick, tick, tick
The clock counts away the hours till morning
And I creep back to bed.   Tim, 10

Adrian Mitchell

'Write to cool down
Write to get hot
Write about things you like a lot'

Adrian Mitchell

Dogs, Banana Milkshakes and other Secrets of Poetry

One of the main reasons I grew up was so that I wouldn't have to go to school. But I sometimes visit schools if they're interested in making magic – I mean poetry.

I'll describe to you what happens on these visits. First of all a school invites me.

I write back to say whether I can come or whether I'm working too hard, writing plays and poems, to do any travelling. (If I accepted all the invitations I'd be going to school every day, and as I was saying, one of the main reasons I grew up. . . . . .)

Suppose I can visit a school. I write and say how much money I need, explain how I'd like to work during the visit and ask if I can possibly have a banana milk shake after the reading. I ask if the children can read a few of my poems and stories before I arrive.

I come into the school at about nine thirty or ten in the morning for a cup of coffee and a look-round. I usually ask if a couple of children can show me round the school. (The teachers are often very busy.)

Finally I am shown into an empty hall which is often used for assemblies, gymnastics, school plays,

elephant training and so on and there is normally a serving hatch behind which dinner ladies will sing and smash plates and bubble with laughter all through my performance. Sometimes I think they must be the same dinner ladies who follow me from school to school. I once had a friend who was followed by an earthquake, but that's another story. . . .

After deciding where I'm going to stand in the hall (not with my back to the light or the serving hatch), I open my poetry bag and take out a series of twelve to fifteen bundles. These are brightly coloured squares of cloth which were painted for me by a brilliant young artist called Jenny Gregory.

I arrange these squares in a semi-circle around the spot where I'll be standing. In each of the bundles I place one of the secrets of poetry written on a post-card, and in some of the bundles I may put a poem or any object which seems helpful. Then I fold up the bundles so that the semi-circle looks like an arrangement of Christmas presents. I begin to feel like a Christmas tree.

The first poem I read is usually a quiet magic poem called *The Woman of Water.*

> There once was a woman of water
> Refused a Wizard her hand.
> So he took the tears of a statue
> And the weight from a grain of sand
> And he squeezed the sap from a comet
> And the height from a cypress tree
> And he drained the dark from midnight
> And he charmed the brains from a bee
> And he soured the mixture with thunder
> And he stirred it with ice from hell
> And the woman of water drank it down
> And she changed into a well.
>
> There once was a woman of water
> Who was changed into a well
> And the well smiled up at the Wizard
> And down down down that old Wizard fell ...

Not everyone understands this poem all through first time, but that doesn't matter so long as they enjoy the music.

Next I point out the bundles to people and explain who made them and that they contain Fifteen

Secrets of Poetry. (Sometimes Thirteen Secrets.) I open the first bundle and display the lovely cloth like a little flag. Then, from the card in the bundle, I read **Secret one:**
Use your feet to find the beat.

What? I explain that when you're writing a poem that has a strong rhythm, like a rock 'n' roll poem, it's often a good idea to walk up and down and make up the poem to the rhythm of your own walking.

To show the kind of poem I mean, I usually read *Stufferation* which is a noisy poem from my *Nothingmas Day* book.

It is made up of a series of two line riddles, each with a one-word answer, like so:

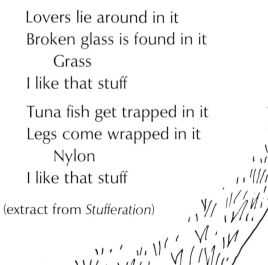

> Lovers lie around in it
> Broken glass is found in it
>> Grass
> I like that stuff
>
> Tuna fish get trapped in it
> Legs come wrapped in it
>> Nylon
> I like that stuff

(extract from *Stufferation*)

Sometimes people shout out the answers to the riddles and that's great. I stomp around a bit during this poem to the beat of the words, which may look silly but it feels good to me. I'm using my feet to keep the beat.

Next bundle – **Secret two:**
If the old word won't do, make up a new.

This means that one of the jobs of a poet is to make up new words, like stufferation, and to prove it I read another poem with a made-up word in it.

At this point I ask the audience to please keep count of the secrets as I'm extremely bad at counting. What number's the next secret, I ask? Three! they yell politely. Oh yes, **Secret three:**
Don't write about *Autumn*
Cos that's the season
Write your poems
For a real reason

I explain how I came to write *I am Boj* (a poem about a fierce giant) to try to stop my small daughters bouncing on me and my wife early in the morning.

My wife asked me to write a poem to stop them, so I wrote this poem in which I pretend to be a scary giant – but it just made them come into our bedroom earlier than ever, bouncing up and down on us and shouting 'Do the one about the giant, Daddy!' Thus, I explain, poetry does not always work.

Secret four goes like this:
Write to cool down
Write to get hot
Write about things you like a lot

I often write about elephants, because I'm fond of elephants. I think they are very beautiful. If there's a blackboard I draw an elephant. It goes like this:

Sometimes people ask me if that's all I can draw. I tell them: Yes, because I went to Elephant Drawing College for seven years and when I came out all I could draw was elephants. Some people believe me. Anyway, I haven't got an elephant at the moment, so in the meantime I write about them. At this point I do some elephant poems. The shortest is this:

The Infant Elephant Speaks

I got a rusk
Stuck on my tusk!

And here we are, already at **Secret five:**
Write for other people, quite a few
Will sit down and write a poem for you

It's great to write poems for your parents or for your friends' birthdays or for your brother and sister. I've written poems for friends' weddings and babies, and funerals too. Sometimes I get a poem back. One day I was working in a primary school in Morecambe and we were all trying to write poems. I decided to write about a small boy called Bevis, a tough-looking, cheerful lad with a few teeth missing and a scar like a seagull over one eye.

Conversation with Bevis

Beside your eye – that scar?
Did lightning strike your racing car?

I jumped off the windowsill, he said,
And cracked the coffee-table with me head.

And I bet you stood up with a grin
Like an open baked beans tin.

31

Well, Bevis grinned again when I read the poem out later that day. Of course I gave him a copy. Next week I came back to the school and the first thing I saw in the playground was a piece of paper being waved at me and behind it was Bevis grinning and on the paper was a poem. Bevis had noticed that one of my shirt-cuffs was undone when I performed my poems. So he wrote:

The Undone Cuff

Was it a cut,
Or a burn,
Even a chapped bit of skin,
Or just for luck,
Maybe a mistake.   Bevis Mulholland

I really liked that poem, because it showed that Bevis was very observant and cared about little things. (Another secret of poetry.) In fact my cuff was undone because I'd lost a button, but since Bevis gave me his poem I often leave a cuff undone for luck.

Secret six:
If you want to learn how to talk to grass
Or dance the giraffe or imitate glass
Invite a poet into your class

And sometimes here I read a poem that I've written with a group of children. Like *Hate Poem* in which a class told me all the things they hated most in the world and it nearly turned into a fight between the boys and the girls but in the end I turned it into a sort of poem.

Secret seven:
What can you write about? It helps very much
If you choose something you can see and touch

And if you're writing about a puddle or a tree or a bust up old car, you should write down what makes that puddle or tree or car different from all the other puddles and trees and cars in the world. Differences make things interesting. It would be frightening if we all looked exactly alike. So you don't spend a lot of time writing about things which make us the same. If you're writing about a friend it's not much use to say:

> I have a friend, her name is Grace,
> She wears a nose upon her face
> She wears her toes at the end of her feet
> And nobody laughs when she walks down the
> street

That's one of my very worst poems and I've written some stinkers. At this point in the performance I often do *A Speck Speaks*, which is a story told by a grain of sand which I made up when I was lying on a beach in Italy staring at sand. It's a long poem, maybe too long for some people. Other people have told me how much they enjoy it, so I usually do it, even though some of the younger pupils and the older teachers may yawn. You can't please everyone and that's another secret of poetry.

Secret eight:
Good ideas often fly off and so
Take that notebook wherever you go

I always carry three pens. One to write with. One not to lend to my daughters. And one to leak in my pocket. And a notebook or postcards. I scribble down ideas for poems, stories and plays while they're hot. Scribble, scribble, as much of the poem as I can get down. Later on, I work on that scribble in a cool way, taking out the words that aren't needed, seeing if the muddle of my first ideas can be turned into a poem that works. So there are usually two stages in making a poem. The hot scribble stage. And the cold carving stage. Here I usually show my notebook and read out a few scribbles and then a poem which started life on the back of an old envelope. *Not a Very Cheerful Song I'm Afraid* – (a silly gloomy poem).

Secret nine:
It's pretty tiring just being you
Write from other people's points of view
Use lots of voices and you may
End up with a poem that turns into a play

This is when I do *Giving Potatoes*, which is a poem about a very beautiful woman who is courted by many men. Now in the old days, when a man went courting, he would take a bouquet of flowers or a box of chocolates. But flowers make this woman sneeze and chocolates make her spotty. What she really likes are spuds. So all her wooers have to bring potatoes. I act out the poem, playing the part of the beautiful lady and all the suitors. The first man who comes courting is, I explain, handsome, strong, rich, witty and young – just like me. I enjoy acting this poem a lot, especially if people laugh.

STRONG MAN:

> Mashed potatoes cannot hurt you, darling
> Mashed potatoes mean no harm
> I have brought you mashed potatoes
> From my mashed potato farm.

LADY:

> Take away your mashed potatoes
> Leave them in the desert to dry
> Take away your mashed potatoes –
> You look like shepherd's pie.

(extract from *Giving Potatoes*)

Secret ten:
Poetry doesn't have to rhyme –
But unfortunately this is question time!

'Unfortunately' – because that meant that the secret had to rhyme. Question Time can be a lot of fun. Usually a hundred hands shoot up and I try and

answer as many questions as possible. The least interesting are what I call the Guinness Book of Records Questions: What's your longest poem? How many poems have you written? What's your shortest poem? Sometimes I'm asked who are my favourite poets and I say: William Blake, William Shakespeare and Edward Lear, but I sometimes add some other names, depending how I feel that day. Sometimes they ask which of my own poems I like best and I explain it's a little poem I wrote when my daughter Beattie was three and reckless, and I was trying to persuade her to hold my hand going downstairs for safety's sake and I remind the audience that if they've got a younger sister or brother they'll know how small people want to act grown-up. The poem goes:

Beattie is Three

At the top of the stairs
I ask for her hand.　　　O.K.
She gives it to me.
How her fist fits my palm,
A bunch of consolation.
We take our time
Down the steep carpetway
As I wish, silently,
That the stairs were endless.

I explain that consolation means something you're given to make up for being hurt – like if you break your nose and your mother gives you a bike. And I make a pause before Beattie says 'O.K.' because she's taking her time to make up her mind whether to give me her hand or not. It's more a poem for grown-ups than for children I suppose, but what's the difference?

I never manage to answer all the questions. Two of my favourites were both asked in South Wales. One was: 'How old were you when you turned famous?' (I liked the idea of turning famous, maybe in the middle of the night) and 'Why are your trousers so long?'

Back to the secrets. **Secret eleven:**
Maybe the search for food
Maybe a quest for glory
But write a poem
With a story

Or a story. Often you'll find that in a story there's a hero who wants something badly. But it's not enough to say: 'George sat up in bed one day and thought, "I wish I had a leopard with a diamond collar". Just then he looked out of the window and saw that the milkman had left two pints of gold top and a leopard with a diamond collar. The End.'

It must be harder than that for George. There must be some difficulties. This is where I often read a story. It may be one of my *Our Mammoth* stories, in which case I'll show the book and produce a furry mammoth out of Bundle Eleven. Or it may be one of my Baron Munchausen stories – stories told by the biggest liar in the world.

Secret twelve:
Pile up your feelings on a poetry plate
Write about something you really hate!

It is at this point that I read a poem I wrote with the help of pupils at a school whose name must remain secret. It is a very beautiful poem entitled *School Dinners*.

Lumpy custard and liver – ugh!
I hate school dinners and I'll tell you why:
There's dog food with peas in, there's Secret Stew
And a cheese and bacon thing we call Sick Pie.

Everybody goes UGH! and the dinner ladies start showerbathing in gravy and pizza-hurling and singing 'HERE WE GO! HERE WE GO! HERE WE GO!'

39

— at least that's what it sounds like. I pass rapidly on to:

Secret thirteen:
To make a poem that lasts a minute
Daydream for hours before you begin it

You may have been told off for daydreaming, but you need to do it. If you really work at your day-dreams and control them you will be able to make them better and better till you're seeing what some people call visions — like seeing your own movies inside your head. And then all you have to do is share those visions with other people, by showing them through dance, or plays, or drawings, or paintings, or songs or poems. I do a poem which came out of a long daydream about a day which is the opposite of Christmas Day, a day which I call *Nothingmas Day*.

No it wasn't.
It was Nothingmas Eve and all the children in Notown were not tingling with excitement as they lay unawake in their heaps.
D
  o
    w
      n
        s
          t
            a
              i
                r
                  s their parents were busily not placing the last crackermugs, glimmerslips and sweetlumps on the Nothingmas Tree.

(extract from *Nothingmas Day*)

Secret fourteen:
Don't just write for the literate few
Write for babies and animals too

For instance I wrote a poem which my golden retriever Polly used to like. I'd put my arm round her and tickle her chest and say:

Good dog
Good Polly
Good dog
Good Polly

and Polly thought it was the finest poem in the world so that I had to repeat it again and again. A poem I wrote for babies goes:

Ring the bell ding ding (pulling the baby's ear gently)

Press the buzzer – bzzz (pressing baby's nose gently)

Knock at the door knock knock (knocking gently on the baby's forehead)

And walk in – O no thank you! (putting one clean finger in the baby's mouth and pulling it out again quickly when baby tries to bite you, but you had better beware because some babies have Count Dracula pointy teeth).

For no good reason I often sing *The Apeman's Hairy Body Song* here. It is very noisy and you can sing along if you like:

Happy to be hairy
Happy to be hairy
When the breezes tickle
The hairs of my body

Happy to be hairy
Happy to be hairy
Next best thing
To having feathers. . . .

(extract from *The Apeman's Hairy Body Song*)

Unfortunately I'm not usually able to do **Secret fifteen:**
To cheer you up when you feel blue
You need a dog to sing opera to you

I call out, 'JUDY!' and from wherever she's been hiding with my wife, out leaps our little Jack Russell terrier, Judy. We sort of croon to her and she throws back her head and sings what sounds like very superior opera to me. And she's rewarded with biscuits. She can very rarely come to schools because she doesn't like travelling. But she has sung at the Unicorn Theatre for Children, the National Poetry Centre and the National Theatre.

That's the end of the main performance of the day and nearly lunchtime. Afterwards I usually spend fifteen minutes with the Infants, doing a few poems, a Mammoth story and a poem game which we all do together which goes:

> The elephant knocked the ground with a stick
> He knocked it slow, he knocked it quick
> He knocked it till his trunk turned black
> Then the ground turned round and knocked him back.
> (extract from *Revenge*)

We hold our right arms above our heads like trunks and swing them down at the ground after each 'knocked' except the last one, when the arm comes up and hits us on the nose (gently but we pretend it hurts). Oh yes, and we turn round when we say the ground turned round.

After the Infants I need a break, so a teacher or two takes me off to the nearest pub for lunch because you know how I feel about school dinners.

After lunch, I work with one class for the rest of the afternoon. First we sit in a circle on the floor or on the grass outside, if it's warm enough. I explain that meeting in a circle is good because everyone can see everyone else without shifting about. In a circle everyone is equal, and tribes usually meet in a circle to talk or make poems or songs, partly because they like to sit around a fire.

I talk about the many different ways in which tribes of American Indians, Eskimos, South Sea Islanders and others make their poetry and songs. They always have a good reason. They make poems which will help them feel braver on a walrus hunt, or poems which will help their children learn how to track down reindeer or catch sharks. They make songs and dances for courting and for making the harvest grow. (Your teacher could find out lots about this in a wonderful two volume book by Willard Trask called *The Unwritten Song* and published by Jonathan Cape – hard to get, but the public library can find it for you).

Then we often play a quiet, daydream game called 'A Flying Lesson'. Everyone sits on the floor, teachers included, with arms at their sides. I ask people to shut their eyes and only open them now and again if they feel dizzy or sleepy. Then I describe to them an imaginary field in which they are sitting, a grassy, oblong field on the side of a hill with an old stone wall running round it except in the top right hand corner, where the wall breaks for a newly-painted white five-bar gate just beside a

twisted old tree. I describe the sky and the clouds and the sun. Then I explain how everyone is growing feathers all over backs and chests and faces and arms. They all become birds and use their arms as wings as I describe how they take off, how they fly upwards, just missing the tree; how they rise up through a cloud, higher and higher; how the landscape below becomes wider and wider; how they see the ocean, far off for the first time ever; how they meet a seagull; how they decide to descend; how they lose their way; how they cross a motorway and get a free ride on the hot-air currents rising from the cars; how they find their field but see a menacing hawk; how they finally descend to join their brothers and sisters in the field and how there are worms for tea. During this flight there are some moments when I describe being in a cloud without mentioning the word cloud and people have to guess what I'm talking about and, at the height of the flight, I leave a long silence for people's imaginations to glide.

The Flying Lesson is a game I invented years ago with my daughter Sasha and we used to take it in turns to describe such flights. They're always different, that's part of the fun.

The only problem I sometimes have with a Flying Lesson is if the room is too small so that people bump wings and get giggly. There's room for good laughs in the Flying Lesson, but you need to concentrate to make it work.

After that, if it's not raining bathtubs, we take pencils and clipboards and go out to the nearest interesting open space on a Poetry Hunt. It may be a park or a riverside or a wood or just the school playing

field. But we all go out and look for something to write about. Each person is meant to find a different subject: a puddle, a tree, a bust-up old car, a bridge, a set of goal-posts, a broken kite, a motor mower, anything. I ask people to explore and write alone, not in pairs or threes with their friends. If they need any help, they are to come to me. Their teachers must be allowed to get on with their own Poetry Hunts without interruption. Some children find a Poetry Hunt easy, some find it hard, but it's not a contest.

Often there isn't time for all the poems to be finished, but that doesn't matter, they can be finished later in the week. Some people can write two or three poems in the half hour or three-quarters of an hour Hunt.

Time's up, always too soon, and we go back to school. There's a short scribbling time in which people can work on their poems. Then we're back in our circle. I give a little advice: read your poem slowly and loudly – if you gabble it I may ask you to read it again; put your clipboard and your pencil down while you listen to other people and listen hard – they'll do the same for you. Sometimes one or two people start saying, 'Oh, do we have to read?' Well, no, I don't force anyone to read, but I do say it's a bit like being on a football pitch, if the ball comes to you, it's only polite to kick it some-where, even if you're not Ian Rush – yet. It's just a

game, not a competition. Usually everybody, in-cluding teachers and me (if I haven't been kept too busy giving advice) reads a poem in turn. When we've heard all the poems we talk about what can be done with them. Could a book of the poems be made and illustrated and photocopied and then coloured in by hand for parents and friends?

Often, at the end of the day, I'm asked for auto-graphs by the class I've been working with. I usu-ally write my name and draw an elephant and add the word 'Peace' on each page I autograph, because the elephant, which is so strong and gentle, is the magic sign for peace. And peace is my wish for you and for the world.

peace

Song In Space

When man first flew beyond the sky
He looked back into the world's blue eye.
Man said: What makes your eye so blue?
Earth said: The tears in the ocean do.
Why are the seas so full of tears?
Because I've wept so many thousand years.
Why do you weep as you dance through space?
Because I am the Mother of the Human Race.

One class liked Adrian Mitchell's stuff and wrote a poem to say so.

> You came up from London with it.
> Came into our school with it.
> POETRY
> We liked your stuff!
>
> You took all your books from it
> We got lots of laughs from it.
> POEM BAG
> We liked your stuff!
>
> For your birthday you were given it.
> Took it off when you got hot in it.
> LEATHER JACKET
> We liked your stuff!
>
> Many a cat was killed by it.
> Everyone was filled by it.
> CURIOSITY
> We liked your stuff!

All your poems are printed on it.
Some are still scribblers on it.
PAPER
We liked your stuff!

You failed your exams for it.
Our mums and dads all danced to it.
ROCK AND ROLL
We liked your stuff!

Lines in your poems created it.
Children burst right out with it.
LAUGHTER
We liked your stuff!

Excitement in the classroom –
Ideas in our head –
Creating, thinking, writing –
We were the poets instead.
For you we created them.
Then we went away with them.
POEMS
Because we liked your stuff!

(from *Cadbury's Book of Poetry*)

Here are some children's poems, written after hearing Adrian Mitchell's poem *What's That Down There?* See if you can find Adrian's poem.

What's that down there
What's that moving
What's that moving down in the dark?

Is it . . . . .
   the hide behind
creeping
   &
    crawling

Is it . . .
   the
     night
        crawler
cautiously
    conjuring
       cackles

Is it . . .
     crookie
      cark
crunching
    cookies

David, 9

What's that down there
What's that moving
What's that moving down in the dark?

Is it an owl swooping down low
ready to snatch or grab?

Is it a fox with soft orange fur
watching the stars above?

It could be a dream of a beautiful star
flying above the sea.

Rachel, 9

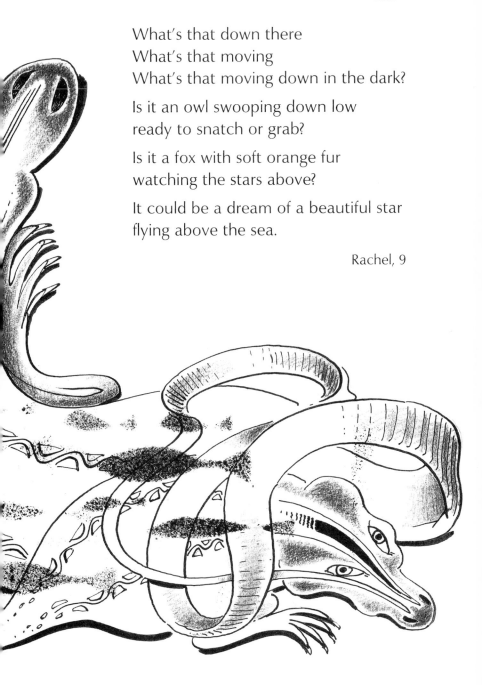

Gillian Clarke

'All the poems I write are true
stories.'

Gillian Clarke

Taking a Word for a Walk

I am told that when I was two or three years old I used to go about stamping my feet or tapping and saying the following sentence to myself.

Ga puts Mentholatum on her sciatica
and Ceri soaks the clothes in Parazone.

Ga was my grandmother. Ceri was my aunt. Mentholatum was ointment which Ga used to rub into her aches and pains. Sciatica is the name for a nasty pain old people sometimes get in their backs. Parazone is stuff people used to soak clothes in to help to get the dirt out. I did not know what any of it meant when I was two or three, but I loved the sound of those big words. Metholatum. Sciatica. And I liked the rhyme and rhythm of 'soaks the clothes in Parazone'. My little sentence had friends in it, the words I knew like 'Ga', 'Ceri' and 'soaks'. But it had wonderful strangers too: 'sciatica', 'Mentholatum', 'Parazone'. (At the moment my favourite two words are the name of the great Argentine football star: Diego Maradonna. I don't know anything about football except for that name which rings and sings like a poem.)

One day, when I was about three, I was stamping out a sentence on top of a wall at my grandmother's farm. With each thump I put my foot down. '*Ga*' (left foot) 'puts *Men*thol. . .' (right foot) '*atum*' (left foot). I made ten thumps with my sentence, one for each brick on the top of the wall.

I am sorry to tell you that on the other side of the wall was a deep, wet, smelly, soggy, squelchy pit of cow manure. The manure (or slurry) was washed and swept into the pit every day from the yard and the milking-shed and, when the pit was full, the slurry was taken away in a trailer to be spread on the fields to make the soil rich and good for corn and vegetables to grow next year. But this day it was full and, when I got to the sixth stamp of my foot and the middle thump of my sentence, I fell in. I felt like a sixpence in a Christmas pudding. They pulled me out and sat me in a pool under a small waterfall. I was soon very clean and very cold, and I cried more than the waterfall did, but it did not put me off words. Remember, always say your favourite words on safe, dry ground.

Words are important. First, they have sounds which give us pleasure. We enjoy saying favourite words over and over. We keep words we like in our heads, on our tongues, to say to ourselves when we hope no-one is listening. Having a good word in your head is like keeping a smooth stone in your pocket to hold now and then, to keep warm and silky with stroking. Words improve with stroking.

Words have meaning as well as sound. First we enjoy them and, after a while, we understand them. One way to understand a word is to look it up in a dictionary, or to have it explained to us.

Think about a word: any word will do. I'll start with 'cornfield'. The dictionary tells me it is 'a field in which corn is grown', and that corn is 'grain or seed'. If you live in a town or city the word 'cornfield' will probably make you see a picture in your mind the colour and shape of a packet of Shredded Wheat or Weetabix. You might see a yellow flag, or a sheet of gold blowing in the wind. You might see a bright square, like a window, on a distant hill – like a field you've seen in a picture, or from a motorway or a train. I am sure, if you live in a town, your cornfield will be yellow.

If you live in the country, the word 'cornfield' brings many pictures, and also feelings. One picture is a square of brown earth decorated with hundreds of rows of tiny green stalks. Another picture is a

cornfield

green surface moving like the sea. Another picture is a pale, shorn square, with all the corn taken away to be stored, and all the stalks made into enormous bales shaped like blocks or cylinders.

Words have another kind of meaning, too. They have meaning that is special to you alone. I live in the country, and when I was a child I played in cornfields. The deep, ripe corn was a golden cave to hide in, to share with rabbits and field-mice, blue and white butterflies, poppies and dog-daisies. Later, at harvest-time, I carried cans of tea to my uncles who were working on the far side of a steep field. The short, sharp stalks of the corn cut my ankles and the cans of tea were hot and difficult to carry. The sun burnt my fair skin. 'Cornfield' to me also means a long, long, painful walk, and trying hard not to cry.

What does 'hot' mean to you? Watch a baby reach out for a tea-pot. 'No', you say to the baby. 'It's hot.' The baby does not understand 'hot'. Only when its fingers are hurt by the side of the hot tea-pot, and it draws its hand away in pain and cries, will 'hot' have a real meaning to that baby. First a word is just a sound. Then each word is understood and experienced, and once that happens it goes inside you, alive with the meaning which your feelings taught you. From then on, forever, that word is inside your heart and your mind and your body.

We all own a magic store of words. With words we can build poems. When I start writing a poem by thinking about a favourite word, or an interesting word, or any word, I call it taking a word for a walk. I write down everything that the word makes me think of. You can do that. Think of a word. Write it down. See where the word leads you. See if it can make a poem appear for you on your empty piece of paper. Taking a word for a walk may lead you to a poem.

I like the word 'pandemonium'. I live on a quiet hill and I like to look at the night sky through a telescope. I read somewhere that scientists have heard a strange whispering in space. They could not understand it. Then they decided that these sounds were the very last echoes of the 'Big Bang' which first created the Universe, echoes that have travelled for millions and millions of years to be heard by astronomers today.

The world's news travels thousands of miles to us by radio, television, telephone and letter. Halley's Comet travelled for thirty seven and a half years towards us and reached its perihelion, its closest point to the sun, in 1986. I've been waiting impatiently to use 'pandemonium' and 'perihelion' in a poem.

At One Thousand Feet

Nobody comes but the postman
and the farmer with winter fodder.

A-road and motorway avoid me.
The national grid has left me out.

For power I catch wind.
In my garden clear water rises.

A wind spinning the blades
of the mill to blinding silver

lets in the rumour,
grief on the radio.

America telephones.
A postcard comes from Poland.

In the sling of its speed the comet
flowers to perihelion over the chimney.

I hold the sky to my ear to hear
pandemonium whispering.

(unpublished)

Poetry is important. It is about the things we all
think and feel. Some of the words we find in poems
are old friends, some are mysterious strangers, and
in poems they are mixed together in an exciting,
rhythmic way.

Small babies stop crying if you rock them and sing
to them. We all love poetry when we are young.
Some of the best poems in the world are nursery
rhymes. I love moonlight. Often, on a moonlit
night, I say or sing to myself this nursery rhyme
which I learned as a child.

Boys and girls come out to play.
The moon doth shine as bright as day.
Leave your supper and leave your sleep.
     And join your playfellows in the street.
Come with a cry. Come with a call.
Come with a good will or not at all.

It did not matter to me if some of those words were mysterious strangers. They sounded good. In my quiet country garden on brilliant moonlit nights I still imagine children coming out of all the houses in the town, and playing in the streets. Of course, I was never allowed to leave my supper and leave my sleep, to play in the streets at night. It is a dream, a poem, a vivid, unforgettable picture in the mind. Without the poem that picture would not exist. Poems can make anything happen. They can make real things in our lives stronger, and they can make unreal things live in our imagination. Poetry is a way of imagining, of creating anything we like.

Young children learn poems from each other. They use them in games. They skip, tap railings with sticks, bounce balls, run, hold hands and dance in rings to poems. As a child I stood in a revolving circle with my friends while one child stood alone in the centre of the circle. As we moved round we sang

Poor Mary is a-weeping, a-weeping, a-weeping,
Poor Mary is a-weeping on a bright summer day.

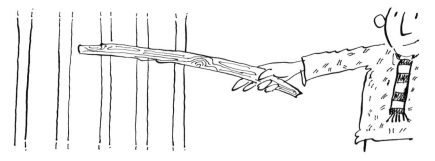

It made me sad. Rhymes are sometimes hundreds of years old. I wonder who poor Mary was, and when she lived, and why she was weeping?

Poetry's a way of deciding. It can stop arguments. If you want to decide who goes first, or who's 'on it', you can dip. There are hundreds of dipping rhymes. I remember this one.

Dip, dip, dip,
My big ship,
Sailing on the water
Like a cup and saucer.
You...are...on...it.

Playground and street games were not written by grown-up poets. They were all made up by children. Although most of them are very old, new ones are sometimes made up. Here is a new song by the - children of Victoria Road Primary School, Northwich in Cheshire. It was made after a visit to a burial chamber in Wales. The chamber is thousands of years old. It is like a cave, built on a cliff beside a beautiful beach. The burial chamber has a Welsh name, and in English it is called 'Apron of the Giantess'. The song has a tone which the children also made up, and it is a clapping game as well as a ring-game.

River, Ripple, Shiver, Quiver,
Apron of the Giantess.

Rock, Tomb, Jag, Knife,
Chamber of a thousand bones.

Flowing, Glowing, Swaying, Lapping,
Apron of the Giantess.

Dark, Cave, Wet, Dead,
Chamber of a thousand bones.

Swiftly, Salty, Shimmer, Glimmer,
Apron of the Giantess.

Ice, Shell, Stone, Slab,
Chamber of a thousand bones ..

In this song all the water-words, like 'flowing' and 'ripple', have two beats, or two syllables. All the rock-words have one beat, or one syllable. 'Flowing' and 'ripple' and 'shimmer' are soft, fluid words and 'stone', 'jag' and 'knife' are hard, sharp words. Words use both their meanings and their sounds to make a poem.

The children worked as a group to make that poem. Then they wrote poems of their own. They used what they had learnt about the sound of words and decided to describe the burial chamber in poems that used only one-syllable words. They imagined what it would be like to be trapped there, alone, and found that to use one-syllable words can create an atmosphere of fear. A one-syllable word is like one beat of your heart. Here is *Fear* by Kirsty Lowes.

Trapped in a wall of stone
Tombs of grey shut me in
The smell of death
The bones of the dead lie
Black fear creeps through my heart.

I think 'fear' has two syllables, don't you? But if you make up your own rules, you are allowed to break them. Does Louise Green break the rule in her poem *Tomb*?

Rain drums
In the dead tomb
Dust blinds me from the edge of the past
Graves stare
Dull, dark,
Cold, dead.

or Kate Preston in her poem *Dream*.

A dream of death
The breath of the sea
Dark, wet
A cell dead and still
Trap of bones.

Sometimes a very short poem works well, like *The Grave* by David Sharman.

Tomb dark
Earth hard
Slab cold
Rock rough
Bone white
Stone dead.

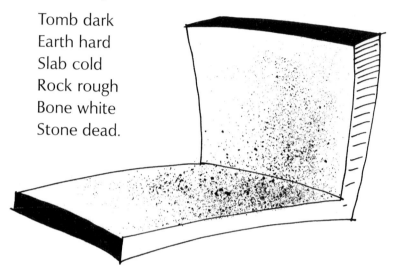

Look out for a two-syllable word in Karen Jane Hughes' poem called *Barclodiad y Gawres*, which is Welsh for Apron of the Giantess.

I walk into the cave
The dark grabs me
I feel as though I am blind
Rain drums on the cold rock
I am in a trap of fear
I feel damp earth
Dull stones that do not age
Wind blows round my head
Death is caught in the air
I am caught in a web of time.

All of those poems are about the stone burial chamber. Next we sat beside the sea and closed our eyes. First we listened, sniffed the air as animals do, felt the stones and the water with our fingers, the wind in our hair and on our faces. Then we looked. In other words we used our senses. You can't be a poet if you don't use your senses properly. Here are two poems written after sitting quietly for ten minutes, feeling and thinking. First *The Sea* by Sarah Thomas.

A branch drifts along
The sea clinging to it
Is the sea drowning
In its own darkness?

A boat flows past
Disturbing the sea
The sea gently holds the boat
And learns to swim.

and then *Waves* by Rebecca Curbishley

The sound of the waves makes tunes
Like someone playing a piano under water
Hinting the rocks to and fro

Black and white keys shining in the sun
Singing notes to white gulls
Waves come up the sand
Taking away stones off the beach
Playing music fast and slow.

You can do that too. Sit with your eyes closed for a few minutes. Listen. Breathe gently. Sniff the air. Touch the textures round you. Open your eyes. Look out of the window or at something in the room. Now write a poem.

Poetry's a way of thinking. Many things that happen in our lives and in the world are difficult to understand. Why are children starving to death in Africa while we in Britain have plenty to eat? Why do great countries argue about weapons of destruction, when we know that we all want peace? Why does a sharp word from a friend hurt so much? Why do we sometimes feel so angry that we hate the people we really love? Why does the sight of young animals, a horse in a field, a fairground, the lights of a city, a sunset, the sight of the sea, a yellow beach, a sunny day, a fresh fall of snow, fill us with puzzling happiness? Why does it hurt to fail, to lose a race, to get a bad mark for work? Why can't we feel perfectly happy to come second when a friend comes first?

If you write a poem expressing your thoughts and feelings, or read someone else's poem that describes experiences like your own, you feel better. Poems can make friends. Even when the poet lived hundreds of years ago, or in another, distant country, you feel, sometimes, a poem was written by a friend, by someone who shares your own feelings. I still feel sorry for Poor Mary.

My poem called *Swinging* made me a new friend. She was twelve years old and lived in the south of England, 200 miles away from me here in Wales. She read my poem and wrote me a kind letter. In the letter she told me it helped her to understand how her mother felt when they quarrelled, and that she had a swing that she used to sit on to think. It was her refuge, a place to be by herself.

Swinging is about a row between me and my young daughter. I forget what it was about. I expect she wanted to do something that I would not allow her to do. Perhaps we were both tired and grumpy, and I got cross about her untidy room. Anyway, we both shouted unkind things, and she threatened to run away. She ran out of the house and down the garden. It was raining and she wore a thin summer dress. Parents don't like to see their children getting wet and cold in the rain, or swinging dangerously on a rusty old swing. Catrin knew that I could see

her swinging wildly in the rain, and knew it would
worry me. I wanted to go out and smack her and
bring her back inside, but instead I waited. It hurt
to wait. At last her rage and mine died down. She
felt cold. She came into the house. In my poem I
describe the feeling between us being like a string
tugging a kite. The kite pulls. The string holds it
back. The kite can't escape. The child runs away.
The mother holds power over the child. The string
is like love, and it pulls them together again.

(By the way, in Wales and parts of England, tennis
shoes, or pumps, or plimsolls, are called 'daps'.)

Swinging

At the end of the hot day it rains
Softly, stirring the smells from the raked
Soil. In her sundress and shorts she rocks
On the swing, watching the rain run down
Her brown arms, hands folded warm between
Small thighs, watching her white daps darken
And soak in the cut and sodden grass.

She used to fling her anguish into
My arms, staining my solitude with
Her salt and grimy griefs. Older now
She runs, her violence prevailing
Against silence and the avenue's
Complacency, I her hatred's object.

Her dress, the washed green of deck chairs, sun
Bleached and chalksea rinsed, colours the drops,
And her hair a flag, half and then full
Mast in the apple-trees, flies in the face
Of the rain. Raised now her hands grip tight
The iron rods, her legs thrusting the tide
Of rain aside until, parallel
With the sky, she triumphs and gently
Falls. A green kite. I wind in the string.

You may know the poetry game 'My Box'. In the game, everyone writes a poem with three verses, and calls it 'My Box'. First you decide what your box is. It could be the sea. It could be space. It could be your imagination. Everyone begins with 'My box is made of ...' You fill the gap with, perhaps, the word 'water', or 'air', or 'dreams', or some other word that helps us to solve the mystery of what your box really is. My box is a plain, beautiful wooden box where I keep my diaries. In my diaries are my thoughts. So in the box is my life. My poem is about the things that make my life: the people I love, the work we do, the house we have made into a home, everything that has made me *me*. I've used some rhyme in the poem, but not too much. Sometimes I think rhyme can spoil a poem. Sometimes you have to use the wrong word to make your rhyme. So my poem only rhymes sometimes.

My Box

My box is made of golden oak,
my lover's gift to me.
He fitted hinges and a lock
of brass and a bright key.
He made it out of winter nights,
sanded and oiled and planed,
engraved inside the heavy lid
in brass, a golden tree.

In my black box are twelve black books
where I have written down
how we have sanded, oiled and planed,
planted a garden, built a wall,
seen jays and goldcrests, rare red kites,
found the wild heartsease, drilled a well,
harvested apples and words and days
and planted a golden tree.

On an open shelf I keep my box.
Its key is in the lock.
I leave it there for you to read,
or them, when we are dead,
how everything is slowly made,
how slowly things made me,
a tree, a lover, words, a box,
books and a golden tree.

A box is a container. Almost anything can be thought of as a container. Here is a mysterious poem by Ayda from Ninian Park Junior School, Cardiff. She wants us to guess what her box is.

My box is made of liquid.
It can be dark and scary.
It stays quiet and still
In a corner all on its own.
My box is big and deep.

In my box there is life and seeds.
In my box there is a shark.
Its teeth are sharp,
It kills everything which dares open the box.

I will keep my box in a safe place.
I'll keep it by the shore
Where it is sandy and golden
In the depths of deep water where it belongs.

Apart from meaning and rhythm and rhyme and mystery and reality and imagination, one of the things that can make your idea into a poem is what we poets call an image. When we say 'image' we mean a surprising picture in the mind. I have just tried to write a poem about a terrible storm. Ted Hughes has written a wonderful poem called *Wind*. In the first line he says

'This house has been far out at sea all night'.

What does that make you think of? What image does that put into your mind? A ship in a storm, of course. It's a house, but the wind is so strong that Ted Hughes says it's 'out at sea'. The house is like a ship. That's an image.

In my *Storm* poem I've used more than one image. My storm sounded like more than one thing. It sounded like a mad orchestra, a herd of wild beasts, a trampling army. Here is the poem.

Storm

The cat lies low, too scared
to cross the garden.

For two days we are bowed
by a whiplash of hurricane.

The hill's a wind-harp.
Our bones are flutes of ice.

The heart drums in its small room
and the river rattles its pebbles.

Thistlefields are comb and paper
whisperings of syllable and bone,

till no word's left, no vowel or consonant
but thud and rumble of

something with hooves or wheels,
something breathing too hard.

You may have noticed one of my favourite words in that poem. You have guessed it: I like the word 'syllable'. Do you agree that wind in a thistle-field is like that buzz you get in your lips when you blow a tune on a comb and paper, and like hundreds and millions of people whispering words in foreign languages?

You can do anything with images. A poet can make anything, do anything, make us see, hear, feel, smell, taste, imagine anything he or she wants. Sometimes, to help children to make really surprising images, I play a trick on them. First I ask them to suggest subjects for poems. In Llannon Primary School, Dyfed, the children suggested The Spider. Then I asked them to tell me as many things as they could think of which are like the spider. I said 'Think of a person who is like a spider. Think of a machine. Think of something to do with the weather, or nature, or your house.' There were many good ideas, like acrobat, architect, builder, electric whisk, sewing machine, knitting needles, God, the moon, a snowflake. Any of them would do but I chose acrobat.

Next I wrote down 'The Acrobat' on a new piece of paper. Secretly I remembered that the children had told me the acrobat is like a spider. The children thought of all the things they could say about an acrobat. I wrote it all down. When the page was full the poem was ready. I crossed out the word 'acrobat' and wrote *The Spider* as the new title. That was the trick. They were very surprised, as they had thought their poem would be called *The Acrobat*.

The Spider

Daring and skilful
determined to dazzle
he performs his tricks on the rope,
turns cartwheels on his wire.

He rides his delicate bicycle
wheels spinning
a tumble-drier
a whirlwind.

He perfects his tricks
walks on stilts on wire
It shines like silver
strong as gold.

He balances to music
drums beating
as he walks
on his hands.

Do you think the trick worked? I do. It is exciting to think of the spider doing all those things in his shining, morning web, just like an acrobat.

Here is a beautiful poem by the six year old children of Glyn-Corrwg Primary School in Glamorgan. They said a snowman is like a candle and thought about a candle first. Then we changed the title to *The Snowman*.

Gillian Clarke

The Snowman

He shines like a candle
and melts slowly

He is white and black
and gets smaller all the time

He is as white as feathers
and white horses and snow
He glows in the dark
like a glow-worm

He stands on a flat place
and makes a shadow in the light

He crumples in a circle
like a circus tent

He turns to ice and slush
like a camel's hump

He runs away like milk
and melts like moonlight in sunshine

In the morning he has gone
like the moon

It is true. You can do anything with images. It is like a magic power that anyone can try to use, and often that magic works. If you are a very great poet, like William Shakespeare, it nearly always works. If you are a young poet, it very often works. Here is a poem by Charlotte Poulter, from a primary school in South Wales. In Charlotte's poem the magic works. She pretends to be something that we can all recognise, and then she transforms the world with a poet's power.

The Sun

I have painted the school in a coat of gold
I have painted the church
It sparkles and glistens
I have painted a house and it shines
I have painted the apple tree
But the apples are green
I have painted a picture-frame
that hangs on the wall

I have painted a girl walking on a road
She has golden slides in her golden hair
The girl walks to school
And the school is a golden box

Michael Rosen

'Writing a poem teaches us how to remember... it's a way of holding on to memories – a bit like a photo-album.'

Michael Rosen

While Greasy Joan Doth Keel the Pot

I haven't always liked poetry. When I was young I thought I wanted to be a writer of big stories. But I do remember my teacher, Miss Howlett, reading us 'While greasy Joan doth keel the pot' (that's Shakespeare) and thinking that was funny because there was a girl in our class called Joan . . .

Once, in secondary school, a teacher said, 'O.K. homework tonight – write a Robin Hood ballad.' At the time we weren't doing anything to do with Robin Hood and none of us knew what a ballad was.

So I went home and I said, 'Mum, homework to-night is to write a Robin Hood ballad.' Mum said, 'Oh, that sounds nice.'

So we sat down, me and Mum, and wrote a Robin Hood ballad. It was full of stuff like:

> Here comes Friar Tuck
> tripping o'er the lea
> There's Robin Hood
> swallowing a cup of wine with glee

Anyway we had a great laugh and I thought it was really good. I was proud of myself. Next day at school, the teacher's there and he says, 'O.K., who's done their homework?' I said, 'Me,' and I'm the only one who's done it. I come up front, hand it to him and wait. He goes through it, and then he puts a tick on it and hands it back to me. That's all he does. A TICK! What is a tick? What's it supposed to mean? I ask you? What a let down!

When I was about sixteen, I discovered you could be very serious (and also very boring) in poetry. I wrote a lot of incredibly serious poems at that time, and also a lot of lovey-dovey poems to a girlfriend. Actually, at the time, I thought that was what girl-friends were for – writing poems to.

Around this time I started to write poems about being a kid – poems like '*I Share a Bedroom with My Brother*' – and the words I chose were those I used when I was a kid.

I share my bedroom with my brother
and I don't like it.
His bed's by the window
under my map of England's railways
that has a hole in just above Leicester
where Tony Sanders, he says,
killed a Roman centurion
with the Radio Times.

(extract from *I Share a Bedroom with my Brother*)

I thought adults would be really interested in this kind of poetry, because it would show them things about childhood that hadn't been said before. They would also find out a bit about how adults treat children. But the people I showed it to didn't seem to see the point. It was just like my secondary school teacher and his tick, all over again.

Later I was a trainee at the B.B.C. and I worked for 'Playschool'. They used to commission me to write things. Whatever I wrote they would say 'Mike, it's super, really super, but what's the point?'

One of the poems I wrote then was about a boy called Ned and his dog Jim. And they met, but they didn't have anything to say to each other.

Down behind the dustbin
I met a dog called Jim.
He didn't know me
And I didn't know him.

Once a kid said to me, 'Well how did you know his name was Jim then?' Some kids have written their own versions.

Down behind the dustbin
I met a dog called Sam.
So I said, 'You look very hairy'
And he said, 'Yes I am.'

Down behind the dustbin
I met a dog called Scott
I asked him where he came from,
But he had forgot!

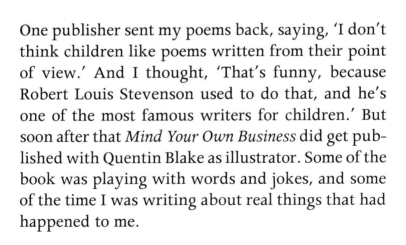

One publisher sent my poems back, saying, 'I don't think children like poems written from their point of view.' And I thought, 'That's funny, because Robert Louis Stevenson used to do that, and he's one of the most famous writers for children.' But soon after that *Mind Your Own Business* did get published with Quentin Blake as illustrator. Some of the book was playing with words and jokes, and some of the time I was writing about real things that had happened to me.

My books are usually about myself, with loads of anecdotes and little accounts of things that have happened to me. If you put them all together they add up to a kind of autobiography: 'My Life'. They are about feelings and incidents that have happened in my life – when I was a child, growing up and then being a father. There's plenty to write about – even ordinary everyday things like trying to put on my baby's nappy.

Eddie hates having his nappy done.
So I say all cheery,
'Time for your nappy, Eddie,'
and he says, all sad,

'No nappeee.'
And I say,
'Yes, nappy.'
So I have to run after him going,
'Nappy nappy nappy nappy ...'

And he's got these little fat rubbery legs
that go round like wheels;
so away he runs
with a wicked grin on his face
screaming,
'Woooo woooo woooo.'

(extract from *Eddie And The Nappy*)

Our whole lives are built out of these incidents and poems help us focus on them. We tell each other little stories about things that have happened to us, who we saw today and what they said and all that. It's how we make up our minds about good and bad, fair and unfair, horrible and nice, funny and awful. All the stories we tell each other have some message like, 'Now wasn't that stupid!' or 'Isn't that awful?'

I've always been a storyteller, gassing on about funny things that have happened to me. Sometimes I tell a story to someone, go home and then write it down, just as I've told it. Other times something starts off on paper, I write it, I tell it, change it, tell it, change it. . . .

I often jot down a word or phrase to remind myself to write about an incident that's happened to me. If you looked at my desk right now you'd see: 'toenail'. This is a little note to myself to remind me of the time when I lost my big toenail. The toenail came off and I kept the nail; it used to sit on my mantelpiece. I had this friend who used to share my flat, and if I wanted him to get out of my room so I could sleep, the only way was to show him the toenail. He thought it was so revolting he'd rush out of the room.

Then, sometimes, something funny will happen. It might be a conversation with a child I know, which goes:

> Do you want an apple?
> No.
> What do you want, then?
> An apple.

Or

> Go wash your hands in the bathroom.
> My hands aren't in the bathroom.

(extract from *Conversations With a Two Year Old*, (*Laura*))

Making a list of 'conversations with a two year old' was one good way for a poem to get started.

Some of my poems are serious, like one called *Platform*, which is about waiting for my Mum. I think it was a very important thing in my life, waiting for my Mum at the end of the day, after school. I've

87

often noticed that children spend hours and hours
waiting for their mums and dads – everyone knows
what it's like.

I'm waiting for my mum.
I go and stand by the
glass case on the wall
where the Christian Science people
put a Bible for you to read.
It's open and there are bits
of the page marked that you're
supposed to read.
I don't understand it.

I watch the woman in the sweety kiosk
serving people.
Mars Bar, bar of plain chocolate,
packet of chewing gum, Mars Bar, Kit Kat,
barley sugars.

Are you waiting for your mum again?

Yes.

I go and stand on the shiny floor of the
                              waiting room
and look at the big dark benches. There's a
boiler in there.
They never light it.
Even in winter.

There are big advertisements that I read.

One says:
'Children's shoes have far to go.'
And a boy and girl are walking away
down a long long road to nowhere
with thick woods on both sides of them.
I'm not waiting for a train
I'm waiting for my mum.

(extract from *Platform*)

You mustn't worry too much about this word 'poetry'. At the end of the day, all you have to ask yourself is 'has something been communicated to me? Was it communicated to me in an enjoyable way?' There's no need to worry about, 'Is it a poem? Is it a story? Is it a film? Is it a banana?'

W.H. Auden, a famous poet, once said that poetry is 'memorable speech'. That's a good way to describe it, I think. That's what I'm trying to write all the time, 'memorable speech'. People often remember poems and think they're worth remembering and can say them to each other. That's what 'memorable speech' means.

You should only read the poems you like. Never think you have to read a whole book of poems. You can flip over the pages, maybe you never read some pages, it doesn't matter. It's not like a story book, you don't always start at the beginning and read all the way to the end.

Poems are great for reading in the loo because you can sit there and read one poem. I used to have a book of poems by e.e. cummings. About a third of the book I never read because I couldn't get past the first few lines of those particular poems. I kept re-reading the ones I liked and gave up reading the ones I didn't understand.

Never allow someone to tell you that you ought to be reading such and such a poem. You've got to read the ones that suit you. We don't write poems so that somebody is going to be made to listen to them. We're not interested in prisons where children are forced to listen to poems. I remember being forced to listen to classical music when I was at school. I don't listen to classical music now.

Remember, poetry is a great way of writing about things that happen to you. Perhaps you want to say that your Mum was angry with you. Don't just write down 'Mum was angry because I moaned and then I went out.' That's boring. Ask yourself what did she really say? Oh yes, I remember, 'If you don't stop your moaning you'll go to your room.' That's the stuff that'll make people sit up and listen. It'll be 'memorable speech'.

A short while ago I read a poem by a girl about the time when she'd eaten the left-over liver, and got into trouble with her mum. She wrote this (her name is Vicky):

> 'Isn't it funny how your name gets longer
> when your Mum gets angry with you?
> "Victoria Glendenning, Come here!"'

Don't forget to write down what you think about the things which people say to you, and what goes on around you. That's interesting writing because it's real.

Of course, people are always telling children *not* to do things.

Don't

Don't do,
Don't do,
Don't do that.
Don't pull faces,
Don't tease the cat.

Don't pick your ears,
Don't be rude at school.
Who do they think I am?

Some kind of fool?

One day
they'll say
Don't put toffee in my coffee
don't pour gravy on the baby
don't put beer in his ear
don't stick your toes up his nose.

(extract from *Don't*)

Some of the poems I like best are the ones which children know and say when they're playing. There are songs I've learned from children, like the rhyme *German Measles*.

German Measles

I had the German Measles
I had them very bad.
They wrapped me in a blanket
And put me in a van.

The van was very bumpy
And I nearly tumbled out
And when I got to hospital
I heard a baby shout:

'Mumma, Dadda, take me home,
from this little rusty home.
I've been here a year or two
and oh I want to stay with you.'

Here comes a doctor. Doctor Brown
Asking questions all around
'Are you ill, or are you not?'
'Yes I am, you silly clot.'

Here comes Doctor Glannister
sliding down the bannister.
Halfway down he ripped his pants
and now he's doing a cha-cha dance.

Anon

Poetry is all kinds of things. It can be mad. You can make up a poem where you go for a walk and impossible things happen, you can drown in mid-air, you can try to eat toast and the toast walks away. Or you can play with words and do tongue twisters, rhymes and nonsense words like 'blimm' and 'cafunkle'.

You can play around with how a poem looks. If you want someone to read a bit of your poem loudly THEN YOU CAN PUT IT IN BIG LETTERS. If you want them to read it quietly then you can put it in tiny letters.
If you want them to read it quickly
youcansqueezealltheletters up.
If you want them to read it slowly
you
can
put
each
word
on
a
new
line.
Or you may want it to slow down and tail off
so
  you
     can
        space
           it
             out
               like
                 this.

Sometimes the way you put things down on a piece

of paper tells you all sorts of different things. If I write
'SLOW
CHILDREN CROSSING'
we understand it to mean 'slow down, there are some children crossing'. But if I write
'SLOW CHILDREN CROSSING' it means that there are some slow children crossing the road!

You don't have to learn anything special to write poetry, it's for everyone to do, everyone to play about with, it's for everyone to write down some memorable speech, something that people say, or could say, that is worth remembering.

Sometimes I play with a word for days or even weeks; I've been trying to make a tongue twister about Houdini.

Who done Houdini in?
Dan done Houdini in
Who done Dan in?

In *Don't Put Mustard In The Custard* I've written something with a kind of jig on the word video.

Video

Oh video oh video
the video the diddy-o
twiddly-o the video
the video the diddle.

I wrote that because the word 'video' sounded to me like one of the choruses of an Irish jig; tiddly tum de diddly-i-o.

Language is not something that's fixed and controls you. You can control language and you can use other people's language, their sayings and make it your own.

In a poem, you can make the words or groups of words look or sound like their meaning.

If you want to say that there's a lot of rain about and it's raining for a long time you can say,

'There's a lot of rain about and it's raining for a long time.'

Or you can say:

Rain raining
rain raining
rain raining

Raining rain.... RAINING.... RAIN
....Raining.... Rain.... raining..... RAINING
rain.... RAIN.... raining.... rain...rain
rain...rain.....rain .... RAINING.... ·
rain......raining...raining.... rain... ·
.... RAINing... rainING.... rain.......
RAINING.... RAIN.... raining.... rain......
..rain.... drizzle..... rain.... RAINING..
RAIN... RAIN.... rain .... rain....... rain...
rain...raining....rain...raining...rain...
rain...rain...rain ...rain...rain....

You can write a poem about an apple in the shape of an apple, or you can make the words, 'walk downstairs'

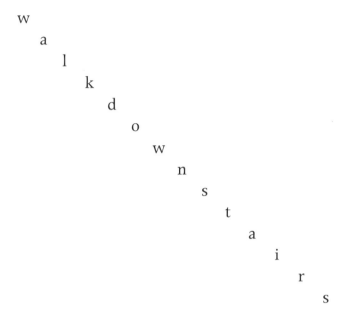

You can make the word 'Eat' have jaws on the lines of the E, or 'shadow' have a shadow, or 'look' have eyes in it.

I suppose this is 'memorable writing' rather than 'memorable speech'. A poem which is made to look how it sounds can be as memorable as a good painting.

Sometimes you might want to write a poem that imitates the way things happen. You might be lying in bed and you hear your dad slam the door downstairs, you might be thinking about breakfast, you might see a crack on the ceiling. You could write:

'I was lying in bed and I heard my dad slam the door downstairs. I was thinking about breakfast when I saw the crack on the ceiling.'

Or you could write,

In bed
dad downstairs slams the door
what shall I have for breakfast?
what shall I have for breakfast?
That crack on the ceiling
on the ceiling.
What shall I have for breakfast?
In bed.

It sounds more like your thoughts, coming and going.

You can make poems sound like you're out of breath, or in a panic; thinking about two things at the same time, or thinking about something over and over again. You can make poems sound like machines – computers; you can make poems sound like the rhythm and movement of animals, or the sea. You can make poems sound like someone boasting, someone laughing, someone being silly.

One of the things I always say to people who are younger than about thirteen is that if you want to write about something that's really really true, don't make it rhyme. If you want to make a funny poem that isn't particularly true, then rhyme is great, it helps you bring together all sorts of funny ideas like road and toad – walking down the road and meeting a toad – or sister and blister. Rhyme sounds good even when it doesn't mean very much – very good for humour. But if you're going to write about something that happened to you, or what really happened to your dog, then don't make it rhyme. Instead you can write it in free verse, writing it down in a way that helps the person read it in a way that you want them to.

Harrybo

Once my friend Harrybo
came to school crying.
We said:
What's the matter?
What's the matter?
And he said
his grandad had died.

So we didn't know what to say.

Then I said:
How did he die?
And he said:
He was standing on St Pancras station
waiting for the train
and he just fell over and died.

Then he started crying again.

(continued)

He was a nice man
Harrybo's grandad.
He had a shed with tins full of screws in it.

Mind you,
my gran was nice too
she gave me and my brother
a red shoe horn each.

Maybe Harrybo's grandad gave
Harrybo a red shoe horn.

Dave said:
My hamster died as well
so everyone said:
Shhhh.

And Dave said:
I was only saying.
And I said:
My gran gave me a red shoe horn.

Rodge said:
I got a pair of trainers for Christmas.
And Harrybo said:
You can get ones without laces.
And we all said:
Yeah, that's right, Harrybo, you can.

Any other day,
we'dve said:
Of course you can, we know that, you fool.
But that day
we said:
Yeah, that's right, Harrybo, yeah, you can.

Some people say, 'Why bother to write things down if you can say them?' Writing is a way of sorting things out. You can do it slowly, you can change your mind as you go along, you can go back and put things round a different way, until you're happy with what you've done. You can read it to someone else and try and find out whether they understand it in a way that you're happy about. Did they understand it? Did they see what you were getting at? If they did, you're winning. So there are two pleasures: there's the pleasure of sorting out something, getting it right for yourself; then there's the sharing pleasure, finding out whether you've communicated with someone, whether you've said something to someone. Do you know how I was

feeling when I wrote this poem *Deep Down*? Have
you ever felt like that?

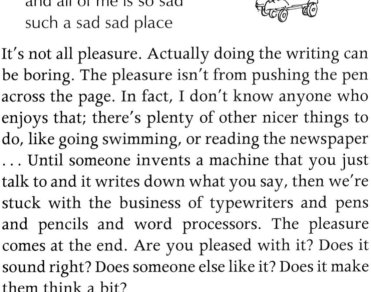

> deep down
> where I don't know
> deep down
> inside
> there's a place
> so sad
> such a sad place
>
> sometimes it fills up
> and it fills up
> and it fills up
> and overflows in my eyes
> and all of me is so sad
> such a sad sad place

It's not all pleasure. Actually doing the writing can
be boring. The pleasure isn't from pushing the pen
across the page. In fact, I don't know anyone who
enjoys that; there's plenty of other nicer things to
do, like going swimming, or reading the newspaper
... Until someone invents a machine that you just
talk to and it writes down what you say, then we're
stuck with the business of typewriters and pens
and pencils and word processors. The pleasure
comes at the end. Are you pleased with it? Does it
sound right? Does someone else like it? Does it make
them think a bit?

One of the reasons why I think writing is important

is to do with television. I think watching a lot of TV is a way of learning how to forget. I mean if you tried to understand and remember everything you saw on TV you'd go mad.

Just think how much information piles out of the screen at us. Every time a shot changes, that's new information, every time someone moves, that's more information, every time someone speaks, or there's music. A lot of us watch hours and hours of television and the only way we can cope with it, I believe, is to junk it as we go along. Forget the bit that came before in order to understand and enjoy the moment that's happening now. I think there are a lot of people who are learning how to forget by watching TV.

Then there's the feeling that TV is about people who are more important than we are. TV is full of glossy 'super people' who are supposed to be ever so clever, the Best of the Best and all that. It can make us think that the things we do are not important, are insignificant, are things that no one really cares about or not as good as they might be . . .

Writing a poem is precisely the opposite way of going on. It can teach us how to remember; teach us that what we've got to say is OK, important for us, and it's a way of holding on to memories – a bit like a photo album. You can put moments down and keep them and enjoy them.

Here are some poems written by schoolchildren after listening to some of Mike Rosen's poems.

Mummy's Orders

Turn the programme off.
Brush your hair.
I'm not finding your slippers for you.
Take that look off your face.
Tidy up your bedroom.
Less noise please, I've a headache.
Stop jumping on your bed.
Time to get up now.
Brush your teeth.
Do something sensible.
Stop crying.
Don't call me from upstairs when I'm
downstairs.
Who left the light in the bathroom on?
Put your slippers on.
It's high time you were asleep.   Libby, 9

Grown-ups Say

Dad says
Don't argue
Be quiet
Share your sweets
Don't play on your bed
Can't you eat with your mouth shut?
No you can't leave the table.

Mum says
Do your shoes up
Say pardon, not what
Don't point. It's rude
Don't annoy your sister
Get out of the shower
Don't whisper
Write your thank you cards.
Parents, they get on your nerves.   Katie, 9

My brother and I play a game.
We put our hands on the radiator,
(Well – just off it)
And we look slyly at each other –
CHEAT! CHEAT! CHEAT!

We put our hands on and grin at each other,
whistling carefree tunes.

Suddenly it gets hot, and we whistle louder,
Screwing our faces into twisty, lopsided
smirks –
AAAARGH! one of us goes thundering around
the room
Blowing on our hands and screaming blue
murder.
After that we have an argument and a fight,
And we do it again and AGAIN and AGAIN
and AGAIN

It's such a *great* game.   Jonathan, 11

John Agard

'The poem business doesn't
have regular opening and
closing times. . . . Maybe poems
come to us because we have no
answers.' *John Agard*

The Poem Business

'What did you want to be if you couldn't be in the poem business?'

This question is from a ten-year-old girl, and it's one of my favourite questions from children, because it's such a sweet way to describe what we poets try to do. The poem business! Thank you Charlotte Briant of Ecclesbourne School for that charming expression.

When it's time to ask questions, children often want to find out about the poet in front of them, not just about poetry. When is your birthday? Which is your favourite fruit? How many countries have you visited?

Once I was even asked, 'are you double-jointed?'

But let me tell you about the time I was showing slides of my country Guyana. Imagine one slide of a very tall wooden cathedral gleaming in the sunshine of Georgetown. That's the city where I was born and the name of the Cathedral is St. George's. It was once believed to be the tallest wooden building in the world. Anyway, you'd never guess what one child asked me? No, not 'How tall is the cathedral?' but 'How many tins of paint would it take to paint the cathedral?'

Of course, I still have no answer. But maybe there's a poem in that. Maybe poems come to us for that very reason. Because we have no answers.

Now, if I tell you that the cathedral is 143 feet high, that's the end of that. Another fact for your record-breaking collection. But how many tins of paint would it take to paint the cathedral? Now somebody has me thinking of brushes and rollers and ladders and . . . wait a minute. Some lines coming. Listen:

> A ladder is leaning
> against a cathedral
> Is God superstitious?

I leave it to you to guess whether God would walk under a ladder or not, but it just shows how one thing can lead to another. From thinking about paint and cathedral and ladder, we've moved to God and superstitions. Don't stop. Keep following those words – paint, ladder, cathedral, God – keep following them like clues wherever they take you. If the words are pedals, your imagination is the wheel. So ride on. Ride on into the 'poem business'.

> A ladder is leaning
> against a cathedral.
> Watch out God, wet paint!

You can try this as a kind of game with your friends. Keep changing the third line but making sure to keep the word God. How about ...

> A ladder is leaning
> against a cathedral
> God likes to smell wet paint.

Finding the right words, finding the line that feels right, this is all part of the poem business.

But I must warn you that the poem business is not like Boots or Woolworths. The poem business doesn't have regular opening and closing hours. Just when you think you've closed up shop for the night and it's time to sleep, that's just when you might get a line or two, or even a whole poem, knocking at your door.

So what do you do? Do you say 'Sorry, we're closed, come back tomorrow?' Well, a poem can keep on knocking at your door so much, you might just have to get up and write it down. It's like saying to the poem, 'I'm sleepy you know, but I'm always happy to do business with you.' Otherwise, the poem might go away and not come back. You lose it forever.

That's why, if you're thinking of going into the poem business, it's helpful to keep a notebook handy – and something to write with of course.

I keep buying the same kind of notebook to take around. It's small with pink squiggles like embroidery. I call it my lucky notebook because I've written lots of poems in this kind of notebook. I usually start a poem on the lefthand page and leave the righthand empty, in case I want to make any changes or scribbles. When the notebook is full, I buy another one just like it.

While working on *Letters to Lettie* and *Dig Away Two-Hole Tim* I had green notebooks with a picture of Miss Piggy on the cover. Miss Piggy must have brought me luck then. Now I'm into pink squiggley notebooks.

The same with pens. If a certain pen brought me lots of poems, I wouldn't just throw it away because it stopped working. If I happen to lose it, well that's different. But throwing it into the bin makes me think that's not the way to treat a pen that's been good to you. Better to stick it in a drawer or some old box of unsharpened pencils, paper clips, bits of rubber, and dead felt pens.

Come to think of it, that could be an idea for a poem.

> My pen travels with me
> bus or train
> my pen travels with me
> sun or rain
>
> my pen travels with me
> land or sea
> my pen travels with me.

That's a start. Maybe you can continue the poem for me. But see what I mean when I say the poem business doesn't have regular opening and closing hours. Here I am telling you about an old pen that stopped working and suddenly something happens. An idea for a poem about a travelling pen! I suppose the idea of travelling came to my head because I travel around a lot, and since I can't drive I'm always rushing to catch a train or waiting for a bus. So the idea for the poem came in a flash, but that special feeling for my lucky pen has always been there.

Often I'll have nearly a whole poem in my head, but I won't be in a hurry to write it down because I want to enjoy the music of the words before putting them on a page. I'll make sure of course that I've jotted down the idea. I might jot down a clue like 'travelling pen'. But it is just a nice feeling to know that a whole poem is floating around inside my head.

And don't forget that people like the American Indians and Eskimos and Pygmies all had wonderful poems which they did not write down, but kept inside their heads and hearts and which they spoke out loud.

They were in the poem business long before typewriters were invented.

If you were to visit my 'poem business' what would you put in your trolley? Well, you'll find lots of Caribbean words and expressions which were first spoken out loud by our great-great-grandparents a long, long time ago. These words and expressions are part of what we call our Creole language.

Exciting expressions like 'duck-belly bike' and 'mouthy-mouthy' and 'hurry-hurry mek bad curry' and 'bambalitty-bambam'.

Children love the sound of 'bambalitty-bambam', especially when I explain that 'bambam' is 'bum' and 'bambalitty-bambam' is what we say when you do something naughty and you are going to get some licks (that's a smack).

Micky Always

Bambalitty-Bambam,
Bambalitty-Bambam,
Everybody scram, scram.

Micky hit the ball so hard
it gone right out the yard
and break the lady window-pane.
He Micky don't hear, just don't hear.

Bambalitty-Bambam,
Bambalitty-Bambam,
Everybody scram, scram.

Micky break the lady window-pane
and when the lady come and complain
Mammy going give he plai-plai
then you going hear Micky cry.

In a way you can say an idea is like an electrical switch. One click, and look! light! But the things that help make up electricity are already there – the wires and fuses and so on. In the same way you help to make up the electricity for your poem by fitting together the feelings and pictures and dreams and happenings inside yourself. You fit them together with words instead of wires. But all it takes is one flick of an idea. Yes, one idea like a switch that turns the light on. But this time the light is the poem.

But something else about the poem business that can be fun is the taste of the words upon your tongue. So if you ever see me talking to myself, it's not because I'm going off my rocker (as you might say), it's just that I'm trying out the poem on my tongue. Waiting at a bus stop, waiting in the laundrette, taking a shower, these are all good places to try out a poem on your tongue. I find that being alone in a laundrette can be quite relaxing for writing and for saying a poem out loud.

A poem like *Poetry Jump-Up* just had to grow like a beat inside of me. You see, sometime ago there was a poetry festival called Poetry Carnival, and that's how I got the idea for a poem on words going to carnival. And carnival, as you know, happens with people dancing in the streets and jumping up to music. So this poem wants you to say it out loud and to shake your waist.

Tell me if ah seeing right
Take a look down de street

Words dancin
words dancin
till dey sweat
words like fishes
jumpin out a net
words wild and free
joinin de poetry revelry
words back to back
words belly to belly

Come on everybody
come and join de poetry band
dis is poetry carnival
dis is poetry bacchanal
when inspiration call
take yu pen in yu hand
if yu dont have a pen
take yu pencil in yu hand
if yu dont have a pencil
what the hell
so long de feeling start to swell
just shout de poem out

(extract from *Poetry Jump Up*)

Another thing children love hearing about is animals. Just one special thing about an animal can excite you to write about it. Imagine fish flying! Well, in the Caribbean and other tropical seas, some fish can actually skim over the water for a few seconds. That's how they got the name 'flying fish'. Barbados is also known as 'island of the flying fish'. And the idea of a fish flying has its own magic just like the eyes of a cat on a dark night. These two things certainly made me want to write about these two creatures.

Flying Fish

Flying fish
flying fish
what is your wish?

In water
you swim
yet like to skim
through wind

Flying fish
flying fish
make up your mind

Are you a bird
inside a fish
or just a fish
dreaming of wings?

Cat in the Dark

Look at that!
Look at that!

But when you look
there's no cat.

Without a purr
just a flash of fur
and gone
like a ghost.

The most
you see
are two tiny
green traffic lights
staring at the night.

Anyway Charlotte, back to your question. 'What did I want to be if I couldn't be in the poem business? A fast bowler for the West Indies cricket team. It's only a thought, but I still bounce poems – so watch your stumps.

Here are some poems written by young people after hearing *Flying Fish* and *Cat in the Dark*.

Kingfisher

Colours flashing across the water.
The kingfisher flies.
After the fish he flies.
Blue and green and orange
Glinting across the water.   Tom, 8

The Panther

Sharp teeth that gleam in the night
as sharp as spearheads
the big black shadow of the black panther
creeps slowly through the grass   Jack, 8

Tortoise

Slow moving through the grass
The tortoise likes to snuffle
Slowly, slowly.
Back as hard as stone
Its head is small and green
Its feet are small and slow.
Slow moving tortoise going
very slow.   Francesca, 9

Guinea-pig Silence

My best moment is when I come home
before my mum, before my sister, before my
                                    brother.
And I catch my guinea-pig called Flash.
I get a carrot and sit down in peace
and feed Flash with the carrot.
The only sound is a faint nibbling from Flash
and the occasional car.
I just sit there stroking Flash and
thinking.   Nick, 10

The Poets and their Books

Grace Nichols

Grace Nichols was born and grew up in Guyana. She worked as a journalist and reporter, then moved to Britain in 1977. Since then, she has published several books for children and adults. She has a daughter called Lesley who writes, too.

Grace lives near Brighton. She likes it there, because it is close to the sea which reminds her of her childhood.

'I remember how we used to go down to the sea wall which runs alongside the Atlantic Ocean in Georgetown. We would wade in the water, sometimes play cricket on the sandy beaches and fly our kites on Easter Monday in the Atlantic breeze. Of course, the sea here isn't as warm as back home, but sitting or lying back on the pebbly beach still gives my head a nice clear peaceful feeling.'

Grace won the Commonwealth Poetry Prize in 1983.

Here is a list of the poems by Grace Nichols which appear in this book, and where you can find them.

I am a Parrot	page 8
I Like to Stay Up	page 10
Granny, Granny Please Comb my Hair	page 12
For Forest	page 17

These poems all from
       Come on into my Tropical Garden (A&C Black)

Tumble Drying at the Laundrette   page 13
I'm a Banana Man   page 14
The Dis-satisfied Poem   page 20
These poems all previously unpublished

Some other books by Grace Nichols

For children
Leslyn in London (Hodder and Stoughton)
A novel for children

For adults
The Fat Black Woman's Poems (Virago)
I is a Long Memoried Woman (Karnak House)
Poetry for adults

Whole of a Morning Sky (Virago)
A novel for adults

Adrian Mitchell

Adrian Mitchell was born near Hampstead Heath, in London, in 1932. He still lives near the Heath where, in a bright blue attic, he writes stories, plays and poems for children and adults. His first play, *The Animals' Brains Trust*, was produced when he was nine. Since then he has been a dustman, an airman, a student and a reporter, but now he spends most of his time writing.

Adrian is married to the actress Celia Hewitt, who also keeps a secondhand bookshop called 'Ripping Yarns'. He has five astonishing children who are now astonishing grown-ups. Adrian and Celia live with their two tabby cats Tabitha and Slumber, Ella a golden retriever and a remarkable dog called Judy. Adrian is the author of the enormously popular production of 'The Pied Piper' which was performed at the National Theatre, London.

Here is a list of the poems by Adrian Mitchell which appear in this book, and where you can find them.

The Woman of Water   page 27
Stufferation   page 28
The Infant Elephant Speaks   page 31
Giving Potatoes   page 36
Beattie is Three   page 37
School Dinners   page 39
Nothingmas Day   page 41
A Poem for Dogs   page 41
A Game to Play with Babies   page 42
Revenge   page 43
Song in Space   page 49
These poems all from **Nothingmas Day** (Alison and Busby)

Conversations with Bevis
Unpublished

The Apeman's Hairy Body Song   page 42
From **The Apeman Cometh** (Jonathan Cape)

Some other books by Adrian Mitchell

For children
Leonardo the Lion from Nowhere (Andre Deutsch/Marilyn Malin Books)
A story in verse, illustrated by Zazislaw Ruskowski

The Baron Rides Out (Walker Books)
The Baron on the Island of Cheese (Walker Books)
The Baron all at Sea (Walker Books)
The Baron in the Moon (Walker Books)
Stories of Baron Munchausen, retold by Adrian Mitchell and illustrated by Patrick Benson

Our Mammoth (Walker Books)
Our Mammoth goes to School (Walker Books)
Our Mammoth in the Snow (Walker Books)
Our Mammoth has a Baby (Walker Books)
Stories about two children who adopt a mammoth, illustrated by Priscilla Lamont

You Must Believe All This (Methuen)
A play for a mixed cast of adults and children

For adults
For Beauty Douglas – Collected Poems '53–'79 (Allison and Busby)
On the Beach at Cambridge – New Poems (Allison and Busby)

Gillian Clarke

Gillian Clarke has always lived by the sea in Wales, sometimes in the city, sometimes in the country. At the moment, she lives on a hill a thousand feet high, with her partner David, two cats called Gwenno and Caib and a spaniel called Meg. Her three children all write, make music and paint pictures.

Here is Gillian talking about herself. 'I have written poems and stories and letters and diaries all my life. I can't stop. I can't stop reading either. I even read the Cornflakes packets, but I prefer novels and poems.

When I was a child, I used to write about a pretend life. I pretended I lived in a mansion and had ten brothers and sisters, and horses, dogs, cats and many other animals. I rather fancied a tame wolf. Now I write the truth, and all the poems I write are true stories.'

Gillian spends her time giving talks, working with university students, running workshops with children and, of course, writing poetry.

Here is a list of the poems by Gillian Clarke which appear in this book, and where you can find them.

Swinging   page 70
My Box   page 72
Both poems from Selected Poems (Carcanet)

At One Thousand Feet   page 60
Storm   page 75
Both poems previously unpublished

Some other books by Gillian Clarke

For adults
The Sundial (J.D. Lewis)
A book of poems

Letter from a Far Country (Carcanet)
An extended poem

Michael Rosen

Michael Rosen was four when he graduated from Tyneholme Nursery School in 1949. Since then, he says, 'Nothing much of importance has happened – except having children, being ill for eleven years, growing a beard and being on TV.' For a while, Mike worked for the BBC and did some acting. Now he writes poems and stories, performs in schools and conferences in Britain, Australia and Singapore, writes and presents television programmes and, with his wife Geraldine, helps to look after their five children – Naomi, Joe, Eddie, Laura and baby Isaac.

Mike says 'When I haven't much else to do, I scribble things down on scraps of paper. Every six months or so, I collect the scraps of paper together into a pile. This pile is called a book.'

Mike has written more than twenty books for children.

Here is a list of the poems by Michael Rosen which appear in this book, and where you can find them.

I Share a Bedroom with my Brother   page 82
Down Behind the Dustbin   page 83
Both poems from
          Mind Your Own Business (Andre Deutsch)

Eddie and the Nappy   page 85
Platform   page 88
Both poems from
          Quick Let's Get Out Of Here (Andre Deutsch)

Conversations With a Two Year Old   page 87
Harrybo   page 99
Deep Down   page 102
These poems from **The Hypnotizer** (Andre Deutsch)

Don't   page 92
Video   page 95
Both poems from
          Don't Put Mustard in the Custard (Andre Deutsch)

Some other books by Michael Rosen

For children

Wouldn't You Like to Know (Andre Deutsch/Puffin)
A book of poems, illustrated by Quentin Blake.

You Can't Catch Me (Andre Deutsch/Puffin)
Poems for young children, illustrated by Quentin Blake, winner of the Signal Award for Poetry, 1981

Under the Bed (Walker Books)
Stories and poems for young children, illustrated by Quentin Blake

The Kingfisher Book of Children's Poetry (Kingfisher Books)
An anthology of poetry for 9–13 year olds, edited by Michael Rosen

A Spider Bought a Bicycle (Kingfisher Books)
An anthology of poetry for 6–9 year olds, edited by Michael Rosen

You're Thinking about Doughnuts (Andre Deutsch)
A novel for children, illustrated by Tony Pinchuck

Hairy Tales and Nursery Crimes (Andre Deutsch/Fontana Lion)
Famous fairy tales and nursery rhymes mixed up together, illustrated by Alan Baker

That'd Be Telling (Cambridge University Press)
A collection of oral tales from communities living in the UK, co-author Joan Griffiths

Everybody Here (Bodley Head)
Stories, poems and games which come from various communities living in the UK today

Nasty (Longmans/Puffin)
Stories for children including 'The Bakerloo Flea'

For adults
When Did You Last Wash Your Feet? (Andre Deutsch/Fontana Lion)
Poems and cartoons for 13 +, illustrated by Tony Pinchuck

I See a Voice (Thames/Hutchinson)
A book encouraging pupils of 13 + to write their own poetry

John Agard

John Agard was born in Guyana, in 1949 and moved to Britain in 1977. He worked for several years as a lecturer for the Commonwealth Institute, travelling all over Britain giving talks, performances and workshops.

John has many happy memories of Guyana. 'I went to a Roman Catholic school, where our English teacher, a priest named Father Maxwell (to us he was Maxy), used to go through the dictionary from A to Z putting words on the blackboard. I was an altar boy at the time and often used to put a blanket round my shoulders and pretend to be a priest chanting. At other times, I might pretend to be a cricket commentator. So without knowing it fully at the time, I was responding to the magic of words.'

John now spends most of his time writing poetry and giving readings. In 1987, he was shortlisted for the Smarties Prize for Children's Books.

Here is a list of the poems by John Agard which appear in this book, and where you can find them.

Micky Always	page 113
Cat in the Dark	page 117

*Both poems from **I Din Do Nuttin** (Bodley Head)*

Poetry Jump Up	page 115
Flying Fish	page 116

*Both poems from **You'll Love this Stuff**, ed. Styles*
                              (Cambridge University Press)

Some more books by John Agard

For children
Say it Again, Granny (Bodley Head)
Poetry proverbs for children

Lend Me your Wings (Hodder and Stoughton)
A picture book, story-poem for young children

Dig Away Two-Hole Tim (Bodley Head)
A picture book for young children

For adults
Mangoes and bullets (Pluto Press)
A book of poems

Pan to Pan (Casa de las Americas)
A long poem, winner of the Casa de las Americas Poetry Prize

Limbo Dancer in Dark Glasses (Greenheart)
A book of poems